NATURE ✿ PUZZLES
Mice are Amazing

**Consultants: Clare Flemming,
Emma Peddie and Betty Root
Written by Robin Robbins
Illustrated by Gwen Tourret and Stephen Lings**

a **Joshua Morris** book
from Reader's Digest Young Families, Inc.

We Are All Mice

All over the world live mice of many different sizes and colors. But there are some things about mice which are always the same.

Mice have long noses that are used for breathing and smelling things. Their ears are big and round to catch even the smallest sound. They have a black, shiny eye on either side of their head.

Mice have long tails, some with a tuft of hair at the tip. Mice have whiskers on either side of their nose to measure the spaces they creep through. If the whiskers fit, then there's room for the whole mouse! Mice hold food in their tiny front paws, turning it around to nibble at the best parts. Their long front teeth can gnaw through the hardest nutshells.

There are five tiny mice hiding in this picture. Use your magnifying glass to find them. Can you match them with the five large mice in the picture?

Match the shapes and name the mice in the big picture.

wood mouse

harvest mouse

house mouse

deer mouse

grasshopper
mouse

Always Hungry

Mice look for seeds, fruit, and soft new leaf buds to eat. They pick juicy berries and gnaw through nutshells to reach the tasty nuts inside. Mice also eat small creatures, such as beetles, snails, grasshoppers, and spiders.

Mice spend a lot of time eating. They cut up their food with their sharp front teeth. Then they chew with the teeth on the sides of their mouths.

Each mouse has two trails. Follow the trails to find what each mouse will eat.

Use your magnifying glass to find two tiny grasshoppers hidden in the picture.

deer mouse

hickory fruit

sugar maple seeds

foxtail barley ears

grasshopper mouse

house mouse

grasshopper

American beech nuts

hemlock cones

A House for a Mouse

Where do mice sleep? Mice make cozy nests from grass, leaves, feathers, shredded paper, or any soft material they can find. But not all mice choose the same kind of place to make their nests.

The wood mouse often digs a burrow in the ground. But sometimes it will move into a nice, warm house. It's hard to guess where a house mouse will make its nest. Although it is often found in buildings, it may live outside in fields and under hedges in warm weather.

The harvest mouse builds a nest up in the barley stalks in summer. But when the weather is cold, it will make a nest close to the ground.

wood mouse nest

Use your magnifying glass to find three tiny mice on their way home.

harvest mouse
nest

house mouse
nest

Growing Up

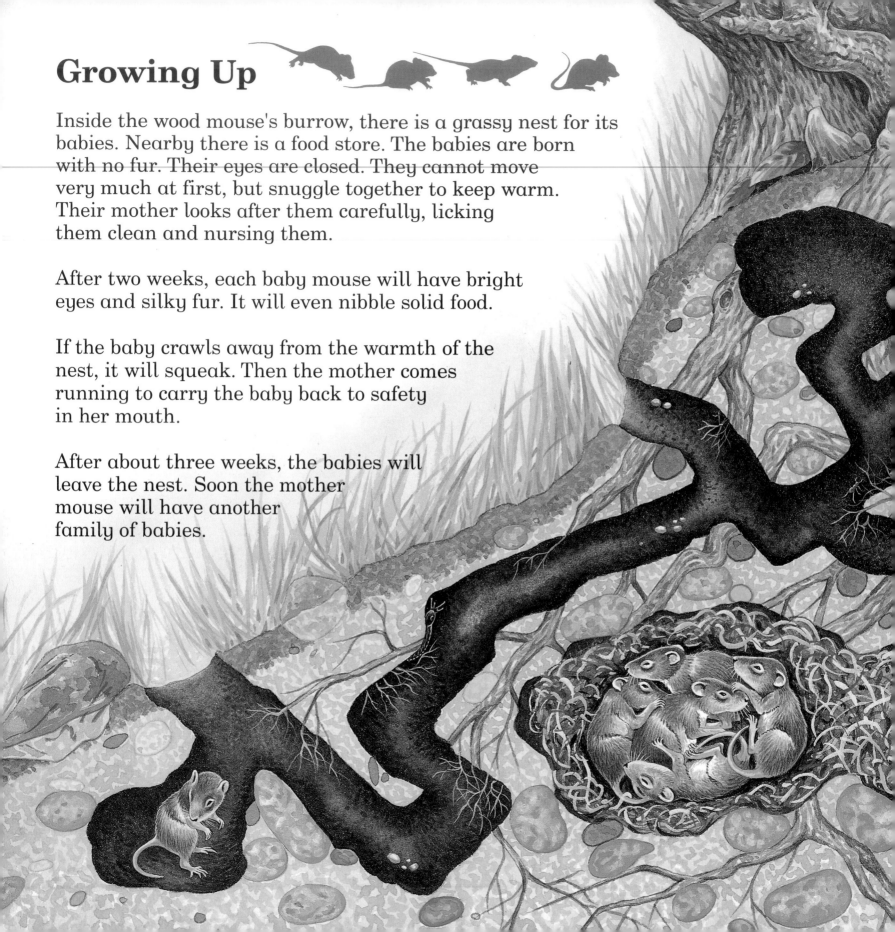

Inside the wood mouse's burrow, there is a grassy nest for its babies. Nearby there is a food store. The babies are born with no fur. Their eyes are closed. They cannot move very much at first, but snuggle together to keep warm. Their mother looks after them carefully, licking them clean and nursing them.

After two weeks, each baby mouse will have bright eyes and silky fur. It will even nibble solid food.

If the baby crawls away from the warmth of the nest, it will squeak. Then the mother comes running to carry the baby back to safety in her mouth.

After about three weeks, the babies will leave the nest. Soon the mother mouse will have another family of babies.

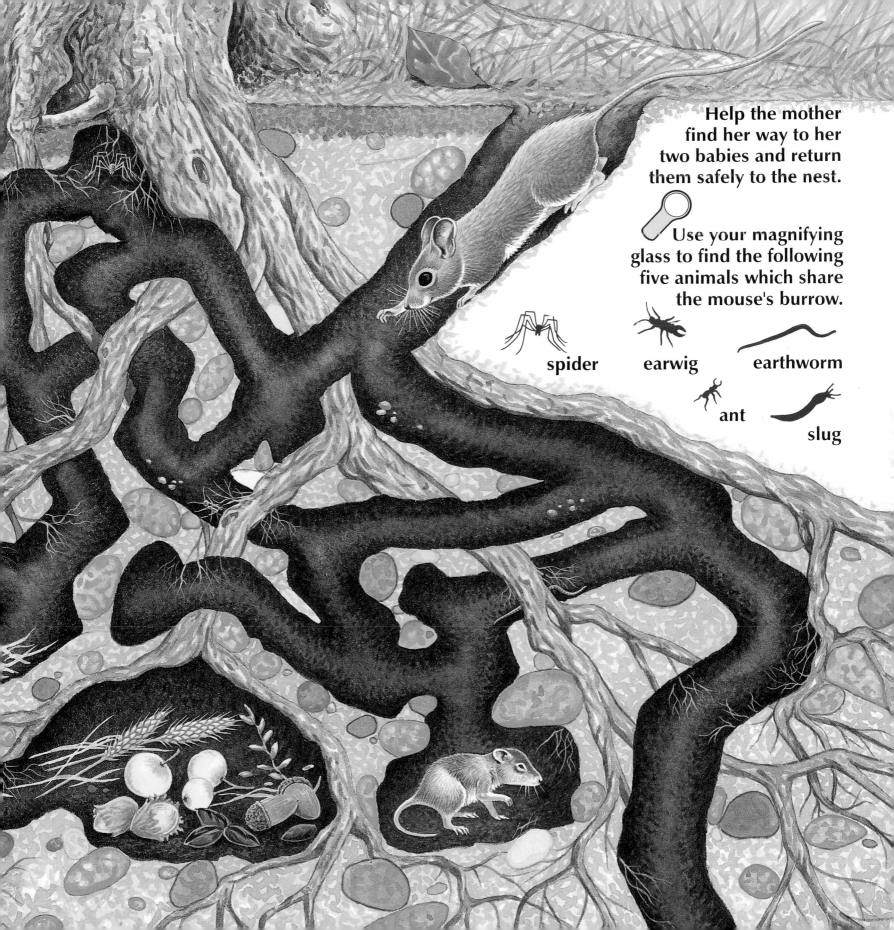

Help the mother find her way to her two babies and return them safely to the nest.

Use your magnifying glass to find the following five animals which share the mouse's burrow.

spider   earwig   earthworm

ant   slug

Night: Time to Wake Up

It is night, and there's a full moon! The climbing mouse scrambles through the moonlit bushes, clinging to the branches with its curling tail. The four-striped grass mouse creeps through the tall grass.

Finding food in the daytime is too dangerous, so most mice come out at night. But they must still keep a careful guard for the smallest sound or movement. Even at night there may be enemies out hunting.

At daybreak, the climbing mouse and the four-striped grass mouse will return to their grassy nests to sleep until dusk.

genet

eagle owl

striped polecat

serval

climbing mouse

four-striped grass mouse

There are six climbing mice and six four-striped grass mice in the picture. Use your magnifying glass to find them all.

I Smell Danger

A mouse must always
be on the lookout for animals
such as snakes, cats, foxes, and eagles.
It sniffs the air for danger and turns
its big ears at the slightest sound. Because
the mouse has eyes on the side of its head and
not in front like yours, it can see what's behind
it — just in case a hungry enemy is creeping up!

Mice try to hide from danger under grasses and
other plants. If they are spotted, they can still
run faster than many of their enemies. The
Australian hopping mouse's long back feet
help it to bounce along in zigzags, making
it harder to catch. It may also try to
escape down holes leading to
its underground burrow.

wedge-tailed eagle

**It is daybreak.
Help this hopping mouse
find a clear path past its enemies to its burrow.**

hopping mouse

**Use your magnifying glass to find
five more hopping mice.**

bro

dingo

mouse burrow

feral cat

fox

Saving Up

Mice store food in secret hiding places for winter, when food will be hard to find.

Some mice store food in their burrows. Others may tuck a little pile of food under a tree root, a stone, a piece of bark, or even an old bird's nest.

gray squirrel

cedar waxwing

fox

black-billed magpie

deer mouse

There are five food stores in this picture. You may need your magnifying glass to find them all.

But what foods should the mouse save? It must choose food that will not spoil. Insects, leaves, or juicy berries will rot, but nuts and seeds will keep for a long time.

When winter comes, food may be scarce. Other animals may raid the mouse's food stores. Then the mouse must forage in other places. If it is lucky enough to live near farm buildings, the mouse may find apples stored for the winter as well as shelter there during the coldest weather.

gray squirrel

cedar waxwing

fox

black-billed magpie

deer mouse

Can you spot five differences between these two pictures?

Puzzle Answers
We Are All Mice

Follow the lines to match the tiny mice with the large mice.

house mouse

wood mouse

grasshopper mouse

harvest mouse

deer mouse

Always Hungry

The two extra grasshoppers are shown in ⃝.

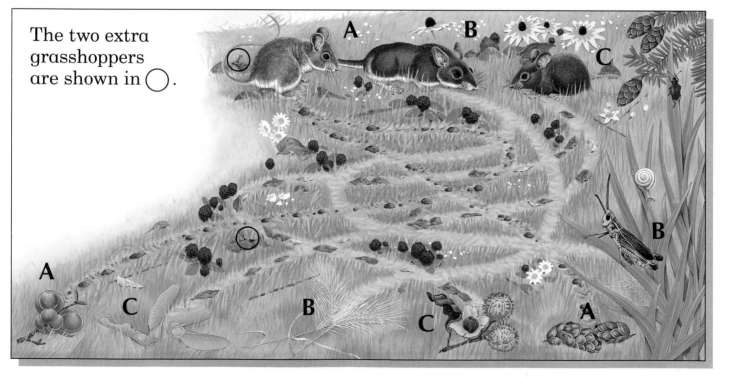

A-Deer mouse finds the hickory fruit and hemlock cones.

B-Grasshopper mouse finds the grasshopper and foxtail barley ear

C-House mouse finds the sugar maple seeds and American beech nuts.

A House for a Mouse

The three mice on their way home are shown in ○.

harvest mouse

house mouse

wood mouse

Growing Up

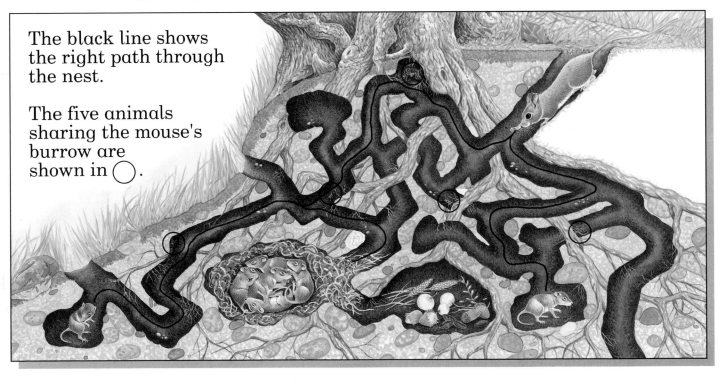

The black line shows the right path through the nest.

The five animals sharing the mouse's burrow are shown in ○.

Puzzle Answers

Night: Time to Wake Up

The six climbing mice are shown in ◯.

The six four-striped grass mice are shown in ▢.

I Smell Danger

The black line shows the clear path to the burrow.

The five hopping mice are shown in ◯.

Saving Up

The five food stores are shown in ◯.

The five differences are shown in ☐.

The 10 mice at the front of the book are shown in ◯.

The five extra mice at the back are shown in ☐.

Did you find all 10 mice at the beginning of the book?
You may think this picture is the same, but there are
five extra mice hiding here. Can you find them?
You may need your magnifying glass.